BARE-SURVIVAL SHELTERS

TRIED-AND-TRUE TECHNIQUES FOR EMERGENCY SHELTER

FRED DEMARA

PALADIN PRESS • BOULDER, COLORADO

Bare-Handed Survival Shelters:
Tried-and-True Techniques for Emergency Shelter
by Fred Demara

Copyright © 2014 by Fred Demara

ISBN# 13: 978-1-61004-182-9
Printed in the United States of America

Published by Paladin Press, a division of
Paladin Enterprises, Inc.,
Gunbarrel Tech Center
7077 Winchester Circle
Boulder, Colorado 80301 USA
+1.303.443.7250

Direct inquiries and/or orders to the above address.

PALADIN, PALADIN PRESS, and the "horse head" design are trademarks
belonging to Paladin Enterprises and registered in United States Patent and
Trademark Office.

Visit our website at www.paladin-press.com.

TABLE OF CONTENTS

INTRODUCTION | **1**

CHAPTER 1
Lessons for Today from Neolithic Teachers—What Many Europeans
Had Long Forgotten, They Relearned from Native Americans | **5**

CHAPTER 2
Shelter Site Selection—Location, Location, Location | **7**

CHAPTER 3
Making the Tools You Do Not Have—
Mr. Rock, the Helpful Hardware Man | **9**

CHAPTER 4
First-Tier Shelter—Shelter That You Wear | **13**

CHAPTER 5
Overnight Wikiups and Ad Hoc Hogans—
Life-Saving Temporary Shelters | **17**

CHAPTER 6
Wikiups and Wigwams—Fast, Durable Shelter for the Longer Term | **27**

CHAPTER 7
Hogans, Sod, and Earth Shelters—Warmth without Wood | **39**

CHAPTER 8
Snow—Brick and Mortar of the Arctic Circle | **45**

APPENDIX
Ponchos and Parachutes—The GI Way | **53**

INTRODUCTION

WE'VE ALWAYS MADE SHELTER . . .
AND THE MATERIALS WERE ALWAYS THERE

The North American continent had human footprints on it for tens of thousands of years before Europeans "discovered" it. The first Europeans of recorded history to visit North America were the unnamed Norwegians who established a temporary but sophisticated settlement at L'Anse aux Meadows, at the northern point of Newfoundland, followed by the probably somewhat later colonies attempted to the south in "Vinland," established by the famous explorer Leif Ericson, ca. A.D. 1000. Both these settlements or explorations predated Columbus by more than 500 years. Even though the settlement at L'Anse aux Meadows comprised at least eight housing sites, carpentry and shipwright shops, and even an iron-working forge, these Norsemen were far from the first inhabitants.

Although that area was unoccupied in A.D. 1000, it had been inhabited by Dorset Eskimo people as far back as 6000 B.C. On the other side of the continent, human remains such as the Kennewick Man and the Clovis Man date back more than 11,000 years, with Clovis points found in mammoth remains suggesting sophisticated peoples lived and hunted here and may have even contributed to the global demise of mammoths and other such species as the long-horned bison. Archeological evidence indicates people inhabited the Florida

1

peninsula some 14,000 years ago. As Neolithic cultures and technology developed from the late Paleolithic and Mesolithic periods, it was not a universal progression that can be tied to a calendar date. Many Paleolithic techniques, such as flint-napping, were never abandoned but were further developed by some Neolithic cultures.

Good ideas were only spread during migrations or other in-frequent contacts among the sparse human population of the time, so calendar-dating a culture only by stone tools can be a complex matter. Stone tools are often studied, however, be-cause they remain. It has been said, only partly in jest, that every stone tool ever made is still somewhere.

Less often found are identifiable remains of early primitive shelter, but when found they do have striking similarities across geography and time. Mesolithic huts found in Ireland are almost perfect replicas of Paleolithic shelters 10,000 years older found in Ukraine. And they are of the same form and ma-terials as were commonly used in certain Neolithic North American cultures until several generations ago. Does this sug-gest Native Americans hailed from Ireland? Of course not. But it does strongly suggest that men of all cultures, of all races, from all time, do tend to think alike when they are presented with a problem to solve and have similar tools and materials with which to solve it.

Consider that when early Europeans and early North Amer-ican natives had only sticks, stone, or bone to work with, they started with their bare hands and made stone tools, with which they worked other native materials into shelter, and, of course, better stone tools with hafts, shanks, and projecting systems. Across the planet with archeological ages between them, with little or no reference to other cultures, such implements usually ended up almost the same. They each, independently, did this like you and I would today: we'd see what worked, and when we found something that worked as a tool, shelter, or food, we'd do more of it and learn to do it better, independently evolving it toward its remarkably similar final form.

Being a Neolithic man in North America or elsewhere

could be a hardscrabble proposition, with no room for the weak and scant tolerance for doing things that did not work. Generation after generation was taught how to do it the old way, because the old way was proven to work with what they had. Not until the "information age" did new technology spread overnight.

And that is the point of this book. Shelter built with the tried-and-true techniques and materials of Native Americans, and perhaps even those who came before them on this continent, still work. Let's learn what has been done before that works, because learning by trial and error may be too costly in a survival scenario. Let's learn to do as Teddy Roosevelt admonished: "Do what you can, with what you have, where you are." This starts with knowing what can be done and then learning the expedient way to do it. Odds are in your favor that these largely forgotten techniques will get you through, even if you start bare-handed. Always remember that those who came here before did not "survive." They just lived here, thank you very much, and they often even thrived. There is nothing but timidity that can keep you from doing the same.

CHAPTER I

LESSONS FOR TODAY FROM NEOLITHIC TEACHERS

WHAT MANY EUROPEANS HAD LONG FORGOTTEN, THEY RELEARNED FROM NATIVE AMERICANS

The first wave of Europeans to reach the shores of North America appears to have been those Norwegians in about A.D. 1000. They brought with them iron tools and techniques for building earth-sheltered houses and communal buildings, such as shop and maintenance facilities for their small fleet. They apparently did not learn much from the Native Americans because, as far as is known, there was no contact.

The second wave, of course, was Columbus and his small fleet, but they did not set foot on the mainland. The first European explorers of the North American continent would have been Juan Ponce de Leon in 1513, but he landed in, and explored, the very comfortable climes of Florida and areas of the south. Because he was constantly moving, he had no need to learn from the natives how to build shelter for himself. He did, however, record how the native people used local materials to built sophisticated and carefully crafted dwellings of cane and reed.

The very early English settlers probably would not have survived had the natives not coached them in techniques of local agriculture, but they brought with them the European tradition for building shelter, from very simple earth-sheltered huts to sophisticated carpentry and brick-firing techniques.

The first Europeans to truly live among and learn from the Native Americans and mimic their methods of expedient, or even long-term, shelter would have been the early explorers or frontiersmen, who favored the environs of, and pursued a living in, the most remote regions they could find. A fair number of these in the 1700s headed away from civilization, due to problems with that civilization, and got along much better with the native inhabitants. When the fur trade burgeoned in the early 1800s, these men, as typified by the legendary "mountain men," drove ever-westward in pursuit of profits, often trading with and living among the Indians, especially during the winter.

Except for European canvas and other textiles, the natives did not find much of interest in European-style housing, but the trappers, explorers, and mountain men borrowed broadly from the shelter-building skills of the natives. Among westward-migrating European settlers, a goodly number had naught in their tool kit but an independent spirit, grit, and hope, and early frontier housing not uncommonly comprised a simple hut to see them through the first winter, during which they hoped to trap enough fur to buy tools and seed the next year. And sometimes while they built that winterproof hut, they lived in the most rudimentary imaginable shelter improvised from materials at hand with techniques that seemed workable at the time, or that they copied from natives, many of whom were nomadic and not enamored of the confines of permanent settlements.

The common thread among all these folks, from Paleolithic to pioneers, is that they worked with what they had, with the tools they had—or more commonly—did not have. They spent no time longing for the nylon tent, chain saw, or backhoe they knew nothing about. They simply took stock of what they did have and figured out the best and most expeditious way to use it in the time they had to prepare, whether for nightfall or winter. This matter-of-fact approach usually worked for them, and it will for you, too.

CHAPTER 2

SHELTER SITE SELECTION

LOCATION, LOCATION, LOCATION

When you are in a survival situation and conditions make shelter a high priority, start looking for shelter right away. The overriding consideration in site selection is whether this will be a hasty shelter overnight, which you will abandon as you attempt to walk out; a longer-term domicile, where you wait for eventual rescuers; or a secure location, where you hide out for an extended period and wait for all the black helicopters to run out of gas.

In either case, the site must offer material to make the type of shelter you need. I hope this volume will broaden the scope of what you consider useful shelter material. If it's just an overnight stay with no impending foul weather, warm and dry is all you need as long as the shelter is large enough for you to lie down comfortably. However, if you anticipate a longer stay with help on the way, the site must offer materials for a more permanent shelter, it must be within an easy commute to food sources, and it must be visible by itself or suitable to accommodate signaling endeavors. Conversely, in an escape scenario, the site must offer camouflage or natural concealment, even against FLIR (forward-looking infrared) or other instrumentation, and offer concealed escape routes.

The site should be free of poisonous reptiles, insects, and plants. It should offer possible protection from large animals, sliding or falling rocks or dead trees, avalanche, or flood. Avoid being in watercourses, even when dry, or likely places for hard rain to run down a hill or collect in a low spot. Seasonal considerations also have bearing: in winter, a site protected from wind and near a fuel supply is desirable; in the summer a site with a breeze will tend to keep insects away and, if near running water, will provide food. If there is a prevailing wind, build your shelter with the entrance away from the wind, and build any fire pits in the lee side of the shelter. For reasons obvious to anyone who by night has laid out a bedroll by an anthill, site selection is always best done by daylight.

Always consider natural formations that provide at least a start toward shelter, such as caves, rocky crevices, clumps of bushes, small depressions, large rocks on leeward sides of hills, large trees with low-hanging limbs, and fallen trees with thick branches or heavy trunks.

Everything else being equal, pick a site with materials for the type of shelter you need for your individual situation, considering the type of shelter and any tools you may have to build it. A good shelter can give a feeling of well-being, which can help to maintain your will to survive—your most crucial tool. And listen to your gut when selecting a location. If a site does not feel right, it probably is not, even if you cannot articulate the reason.

CHAPTER 3

MAKING THE TOOLS YOU DO NOT HAVE

MR. ROCK, THE HELPFUL HARDWARE MAN

Making ad hoc stone tools to pound, chop, or cut does not require a great deal of skill, or even time. One of the hallmarks of Paleolithic tools is that they are crude, as they were made quickly to be used and then discarded. In the Mesolithic and Neolithic periods, workmen took a lot more time to make their tools, and although many were lost or broken, they were not generally discarded or left behind. Specialized toolmakers became some of the earliest industrialists, and materials and finished tools some of the first items of commerce. Many times such tools were highly enough regarded that they were buried with their owner, with the thought they might be needed later. (In my case, a small shovel might be thoughtful, just in case the undertaker got ahead of himself.) Since we're amateur toolmakers, we will go with the Paleolithic plan of the quick-and-dirty tool. Although, if we get lucky and make a particularly good one, it might be worth packing along.

The first tool was probably a hammer in the form of a stick or bone, or rock A used to break rock B, in hopes of getting a sharp edge that would serve as a knife or be suitable for chopping. Fine-grained igneous or metamorphic rocks will probably give the best results, as sedimentary rocks are generally too soft. As a rule, any rock that gives a conchoidal fracture will make a tool; men of skill can work cryptocrystalline rocks (such as chalcedony, agate, jasper, flint, or obsidian) into very fine tools. If there is a stream, look in it for rocks that are hard

9

enough to have retained an angular shape. Generally, if you can break a flat, palm-sized rock along its longest plane, you will have at least one edge that will serve as, or can be dressed into, a palm knife/scraper edge. Another technique is to heat the rock in the fire and dump it into cold water so it will shatter, or selectively pour water on one side. Breaking rocks in these crude manners yields uneven and unpredictable results, but the resulting shapes will suggest their use: cutting, scraping, chopping, or digging.

The second level of stone technology was used from about a million and a half years to half a million years ago, depending on which part of the earth you are studying and whose numbers you find credible. These have been named Acheulean archeological cultures. By then, the toolmaker knew what he wanted, could visualize the tool that was inside the stone, and developed the skills to remove all parts of that stone that did not look like that tool. These are generally called "core tools."

From a Lower Paleolithic site at Cintegabelle, Haute-Garonne, France, this very early tool shows evidence of purposeful shaping. The earliest stone tools are called Oldowan and date to a couple million years ago. Although it is not known who made and used them, it is apparent they took an existing stone of roughly the right size and shape, hit it a couple licks, and hoped for the best. Photo: Courtesy Wikipedia.

As shown on the previous page, they still often started with a fortuitously shaped rock. And why not?

Such tools of opportunity, for our purpose here, would probably be best made by finding a smooth-grained stone, striking it on the thin side, and hoping to cause a flaking fracture with a sharp edge that would serve as a palm knife or scraper. An unhafted hand ax would be the same but bigger and would be useful for chopping or weakening breakable limbs or poles for hasty shelter. Note that even a stone ax without a handle can be used for serious chopping by using an appropriate stout stick or root cudgel to pound it through the workpiece, as you would "baton" a conventional knife or a shake-maker's froe. The operational word in this context is "hasty," but hasty does not have to mean ineffective.

Aboriginal people the world over have primarily used sticks for digging and have found that bones—such as shoulder blades or jawbones—can be quite effective diggers. For carrying soil, a bark container or crude basket often served them well. The lesson is that not only are the materials you need for shelter there but also the materials needed to make tools to more effectively work with those building materials.

CHAPTER 4

FIRST-TIER SHELTER

SHELTER THAT YOU WEAR

The earliest men, even among nomadic cultures in temperate regions, had to come up with shelter from the elements. Simple but clever adaptations for improvised clothing often proved sufficient, as did taking advantage of existing shelter, like the protection of spreading trees or natural caves.

Aboriginal, opportunistic methods of shelter are worth knowing in advance of a survival scenario because when things are not going your way, you may have to "do what you can with what you have."

Depending on your location, you must keep warm, stay cool, and block the damaging radiation and blinding light of the sun. In some venues, all three can become important at different times of day. Once fire became man's ally, it greatly enhanced keeping warm and was a significant step in realizing that we could, for better or worse, change the world around us. When improvised Paleolithic stone implements became part of man's tool kit, they opened new possibilities for using local materials in quickly improvised, or permanent, shelter. Protection from heat is largely a matter of staying hydrated and avoiding direct sun. In most regions, however, keeping warm is the larger consideration.

We'll use the "fell naked from a plane" scenario as a baseline and assume that what you have to work with for shelter is what nature provides and what you brought between your ears. If you happen to have a knife, a Bic to flick, good boots, a shelter half or space blanket, and a canteen, you can probably consider yourself a "tourist" and not a "survivor." The aboriginal techniques we will review can be done starting with no tools. Because the more likely scenario is that you will have at least a knife, I will also review some of the more modern techniques that assume you may have some modern materials— just don't despair if you are bare-handed, as the ancients did not. If you have a friend to share the experience, that's good news, too—if nothing more, at least it means that only one of you will starve to death.

You can either improvise wearable protection on your person or build immobile shelter to use and leave. Many basic materials work for either. Wearable shelter implies you plan to keep moving, and such shelter is just crude clothing. There are few wilderness opportunities for "cloth," although if you plan to sit a while you can weave ugly but serviceable hats and cloaks from reeds, grasses, and strips of bark. The best fibers you are likely to find in North America are the papery inner bark on dead maple and similar trees, the fibrous stalks of plants like dead nettles, shredded cedar or sage bark, or desert yucca fiber. All were used by aboriginal peoples. Flat reeds and grasses, cattails leaves, yucca leaves, and the like weave into quickly improvised hats and serape-type mats to keep the sun off. Scrounge the materials available where you are and make what you need to protect from local elements. Even soft evergreen branches readily fashion into improvised sun hats. Bark that will slip—birch, willow, cascara—can be easily shaped into emergency hats, as can large leaves, such as skunk cabbage or whatever is native to where you are.

Some of the best textile-grade bark is the inner bark of the red or yellow "cedar" trees of the Thuja genus (there are no true cedars in North America; what gets called cedar is usually in the *Thuja* or *Juniperus* family).

Cedar bark may be one of the best examples of bark as clothing, as it is easily harvested and simply used to make a very high-quality textile. Historically, natives in the Pacific Northwest made most of their clothing from this material,

These native girls on Vancouver Island wear dresses woven from strips of inner cedar bark, which they peel more from a tree. Drawing by J. Semeyn, from *Indian Legends of Vancouver Island* by Alfred Carmichael, via Wikipedia.

with animal skins a secondary material. After the bark was peeled in long strips from the trees, the outer layer was split away, and the soft flexible inner layer was often shredded and processed into felt-like strips, which could be sewn or woven into a variety of fabrics that were either dense and watertight or soft and comfortable. Women wore skirts and capes of red-cedar bark, while men wore long capes.

In an extemporaneous setting, a lower-quality but functional product can be simply made by peeling away the slivery outer bark (save for tinder) and weaving inside strips as needed. Many different types of bark can be used for clothing or useful items if worked while still green and flexible.

Animal skins usually make superior expedient clothes; so if there is game present and you have a weapon, go for it. Men have survived blizzards by shooting large animals (such as caribou or bison), slitting them open, and crawling inside. A rabbit killed with a thrown stick will yield, bare-handedly, skin to make a hat or wrap your feet. A snake's skin, beheaded with a sharp rock and turned inside out, is cordage to wrap or bind. And inside is lunch. Not lunch? Then you're not hungry yet. Remember: if you have water, drink before you are thirsty; if you have food, eat before you are starving.

If you have conventional clothes, stuffing them with available insulation makes a world of difference. Ask any wino under a bridge with newspaper stuffed in his shirt and pants. Cattail fluff not only makes number-one tinder but insulation as well. It was used for quilt batting in China for ages. Consider also moss, leaves, and grasses.

CHAPTER 5

OVERNIGHT WIKIUPS AND AD HOC HOGANS

LIFE-SAVING TEMPORARY SHELTERS

As older kids after World War II, a buddy and I spent several days in the deep woods, on purpose, with one mail-order "bowie" knife and a couple books of penny matches between us. We had Levi jackets, decent boots, slouch hats, and nothing else. Except for a muzzle-loader, we really were about as well equipped as the early explorers and trappers. We were just having fun taking our time from point A to point B overland through timber country, but those early mountain men were on their own for months at a time, covering a lot of ground, usually with a job to do well beyond "surviving."

The old-timers understood that the aboriginal people who came there ahead of them did not "survive"; they just skillfully adapted to living there, without making a big fuss. When it came to practical things, like quick shelter, these first Europeans learned freely from the natives. And so can we. Bud and I were raised in the woods and were in no hurry, and so had time to hypothesize over a campfire and try things we'd read or dreamed up or been told. Everything we tried that worked, we later learned, had been done before. We wove blanket mats of sword fern and cedar boughs, slept damp but warm on a bed of duff under fir and cedar trees, and ate whatever moved slowly. It's not that hard to get along in the wilderness, if you do it like those who came before—not as an exercise in survival, but just in living like everybody else did, as adaptable hunter-gathers, long before we perfumed princes from Europe happened on the scene.

There are many techniques we can borrow from early American cultures on the general topic of shelter in unplanned wilderness living ("survival" to you city kids). The simplicity of their methods illustrates the most important aspect of all: the importance of knowing you can do it and having decided that you will do it and then getting on with it. You may lack particular skills that early folks had developed, but if you know that everything you need will probably be there (not easy but there), you can make it home. Unless you decide it's a better life there and you decide to stay, of course.

EMERGENCY SHELTER

"Emergency" implies you need shelter quickly and you don't have much with which to work. Even burrowing into the snow greatly increases your odds of survival; digging a cave in

Natural rock shelters or caves are intuitive instant shelter—and they are readily and quickly enhanced by using nearby rubble to fully or partly enclose them. The floor may be quickly enhanced by the addition of leaves, duff, grasses, ferns, or boughs for comfort or insulation. Even a shallow indent in a cliff may be a good starting point for expedient shelter. Photo: Wikipedia.

a snow bank is even better (see Chapter 8). Get out of the wind. If you're in the woods and darkness is upon you, even a deer bed of moss, leaves, ferns, grasses, or evergreen boughs into which you can crawl will go a long way toward keeping you from dying of hypothermia before daylight. Even if you are wet, keeping the wind off may by itself save you from hypothermia. Ignore stickers and bugs; they come with the territory. If you have an hour or so of daylight to prepare shelter in the woods, you may even have time to get comfortable.

Building quick shelters is not rocket science. It is intuitive but does take common sense. Native Americans and aboriginal people everywhere survived, and often thrived, because of their wealth of common sense, and backbone. People in any situation, if blessed with these same qualities, can do the same.

TRENCHES AND HIDES:
DIGGING IN BUT NOT VERY DEEP

Being on your own in the wilderness—cold, wet, and hungry—is not a good situation, but it is one you can largely control. What's for dinner has been addressed in other books (including my two, *Eating on the Run* and *Survival Guide to Edible Insects*), so in this context we'll just note that battling hypothermia takes a lot of calories. Thus, I'll address shelter first.

Even a deer likes a comfortable bed, and depending on your situation, a shallow depression or trench not much bigger than shoulder-width will suffice for overnight. Depending on whether you are in snow, woods, or desert sand, dig down just deep enough that you can roll over, as wide as you are, with an additional shallow depression for your buttocks and shoulders. Line it with 6 inches or so of grass, leaves, ferns, or evergreen boughs as dry as you can find. More is better.

Keep in mind that when at rest, according to Department of Defense studies, up to 80 percent of your body heat loss can be into the ground. Weave a cover for your trench from sticks or boughs or, if you anticipate rain, make the cover with a slight peak on one side to shed water and cover it well with additional thatch of leaves, duff, or boughs. If dry weather is certain, a "blanket" woven from several layers of fern, reeds, or grass may suffice to keep the wind off. If snow is in your future, build the hidey hole with a good layer of snow, over a shallow roof that will support it, and fashion a way to block the entrance. Build small because body heat can be significant. The following are some ideas from military manuals, but think outside the box and adapt to your particular situation.

Using the same principle that has worked for quiggly holes and modern earth-sheltered homes, a hasty shelter the size of a large coffin can be quickly dug into snow, soil, or sand, and covered with what is at hand. First scoop down (or scrape into a surrounding/sheltering low wall if digging is too hard) to form "walls" and then overlay this with sticks for a framework. Then overlay with foliage or grass that is capped with soil, sand, or snow. With an improvised door, such a shelter keeps off the wind and cold. It also protects from the heat and sun in the other extreme. The only tool required is a digging stick or a sharp rock—and not even this to build a shade shelter in sand.

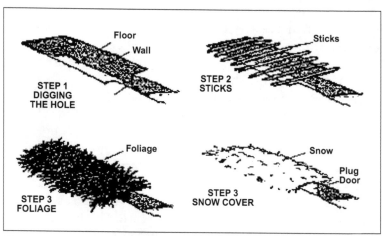

Shallow shelter can be dug into snow, soil, or sand and covered with what you have available. Drawing: *U.S. Army Survival Manual*, FM 21-76.

A "beach" shade shelter serves in any sandy location where you have to get out of the sun. A beach is more likely to be a source of hasty materials. Simply pick a site above high tide and use driftwood to scoop out a trench, using that to raise the sides for more room. Line this with suitable material (even dry sand), overlay a frame of driftwood, and continue to cover with available materials. Drawing: FM 21-76.

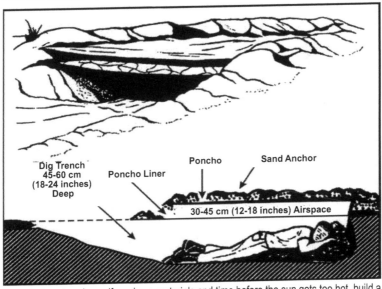

Dig Trench 45-60 cm (18-24 inches) Deep

Poncho Liner

Poncho

Sand Anchor

30-45 cm (12-18 inches) Airspace

In harsh desert environs, if you have materials and time before the sun gets too hot, build a double-layered cover as insulation. It may be to your benefit to seek natural shade rather than work in the debilitating heat, but a simple shade shelter such as this can reduce midday heat by 30 to 40 degrees. Drawing: FM 21-76.

FAST AND TEMPORARY SHELTER

For a Huck Finn or Robinson Crusoe style of temporary shelter, you must strike a balance between what there is to work with and what you need to prepare for. Like these fictional characters, take stock of what you have and, while you are doing that, get busy hoarding what will be useful. Start with material for a deer bed in case you get interrupted or lose light, and go on from there. Dry is always better (even crucial except in the tropics) because of water's heat-robbing quality. Your body heat will often dry clothing but not if you continually get resoaked. Planning on using body heat to dry all the water that might come your way is only doable if you never stop moving, which may not be feasible. You may not have the calories to waste, and you must rest. Thus, some sort of a roof and windbreak is important. Build it away from the wind, with no danger of water running in.

Green evergreen boughs and leafy hardwood limbs that can be hand broken and that are suitable for weaving or layering will probably be the most expeditious. If you have a large log, a sturdy low branch a few feet off the ground, or a fallen tree, it makes a good foundation on which to build. Don't make it too steep, as gravity will play a big part in keeping your shelter together—although the steeper it is, everything else being equal, the better it will shed water. Large evergreen trees may have large limbs close to the ground as a good starting point. With nothing to build on, three forked sticks stacked in a tripod (or more sticks stacked in a circle) make a good foundation. Just like stacking rifles in the army, build in a shallow cone. Forked sticks intertwined at the top, along with gravity, can often make up for a lack of lashing material. Improvised lashing material, if necessary, can come in the form of yucca or buffalo grass leaves, strongly fibrous bark, or fibrous root of such plants as mallow.

Once you have the horizontal "bones" in place, whether as a lean-to from a log or dirt bank or as a stand-alone, weave evergreen boughs or green hardwood limbs through these horizontally—in effect, building an inverted basket. Leave an entrance, but no bigger than you need. Once completed you have a basic windbreak, but you want it dry. This kind of shelter is not waterproof, but the right thatch overlay can turn the water, encouraging it to run down and away and not drip on you. A thick layer of evergreen boughs, stem up, woven into the "basket" starting at the bottom and working toward the top, works surprisingly well. Large handfuls of grass or reeds, woven in vertically, in overlapping layers from bottom up, are what have kept European thatch houses bone dry for centuries.

Assuming the structure you built is strong enough, the more cover you add, the better it will be. You can often slide both forearms under large swatches of duff from the forest floor and get "tiles" of leaves or needles to overlay your wee

The U.S. Army calls this by the unappreciative name of a "debris hut," but for speed and warmth it's hard to beat. If you find downed trees in the woods, you are already off to a good start. If you build a door and give yourself plenty of ground insulation, you will find it surprisingly comfy. If you anticipate wind, be sure to anchor top layers with heavy material. Drawing: FM 21-76.

The crude hut illustrated here was found at Terra Amata, near Nice, France, and was dated to the Mindel Glaciation, some 380,000 years ago. Such a shelter would have been quickly built for one-time use by hunter-gathers passing through. The technique of anchoring the bottoms of the reeds or brush with stones was used in Native American wikiups. Drawing: Wikipedia.

hut. Bark from dead trees, especially large, rotten evergreen logs, can often be removed in newspaper-size pieces to also make excellent "sheet goods" for constructing or covering. With or without hope of a warming fire, a "blanket" in a simple square-weave pattern of ferns or fine evergreen boughs will make a big difference. A door can be built in the same way, just smaller and heavier.

When in the final "insulating" stages of your shelter, keep in mind that the material you will use will settle and you want it to repel water. For these reasons, pile it as deep as you judge the supporting structure will hold, with a pattern designed for the cover to act as thatch to direct the water to the sides. As long as the structure you build is sound and presents no danger of collapsing on you, there is no such thing as too much insulation or cover; the same goes for dry bedding inside.

CHAPTER 6

WIKIUPS AND WIGWAMS

FAST, DURABLE SHELTER FOR THE LONGER TERM

A seasonal or temporary native shelter we can easily mimic is the wikiup, built with a framework as described previously but larger and covered with woven brush, reeds, grass, or other local material. The next step up is the wigwam, halfway between a wikiup and a tepee, with an ad hoc framework, but covered with reusable mats or skins. The final evolution is the tepee, with reusable mats or hides as cover but built on a conical circle of tall poles, designed to be knocked down and moved for reuse. With materials at hand, a crude wikiup is fast and serves our purpose.

In *An Apache Life-Way: The Economic, Social, and Religious Institutions of the Chiricahua Indians*, Morris Opler wrote:

> The home in which the family lives is made by the men and is ordinarily a circular, dome-shaped brush dwelling, with the floor at ground level. It is eight feet high at the center and approximately seven feet in diameter. To build it, long fresh poles of oak or willow are driven into the ground or placed in holes made with a digging stick. These poles, which form the framework, are arranged at one-foot intervals and are bound together at the top with yucca-leaf strands. Over them a thatching of bundles of big bluestem grass or bear grass is tied, shingle style, with yucca strings. A smoke hole opens above a central fireplace. A hide, suspended at the entrance, is fixed on a cross-beam so that it may be swung for-

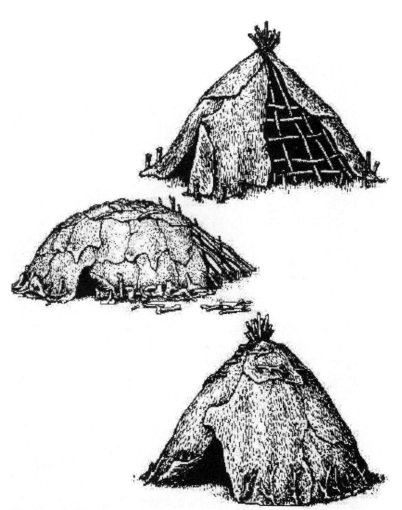

Mousterian dwellings from a culture in the Ukraine 44,000 years ago showed building techniques of a domed framework covered with animal skins (center), also found in Ireland in Mesolithic times—and in North America 200 years ago. An Upper Paleolithic structure from the same area 13,000 ago used a steep pyramid, interwoven wood supports, and animal skin covering (top). A round-based cone structure, again from the same area, was almost tepee like, and covered with animal skins. These latter two designs were common among North American natives as wigwams, where the skins would be taken when they moved, and a new framework built. The tepee, which was designed to be moved completely, evolved from this concept. Such frameworks have been used all over, and covered with what was at hand. Sometimes, the covering and the framework are one and the same depending on the available material. Drawings: Vortex Archives.

Provided you have straight, uniform components, in this case tule reeds used by the Jua-neno tribes near what is now San Diego, this sort of wikiup goes up quickly and makes a tidy shelter with scant need for additional thatch. Such components also lend themselves to weaving into coarse mats, or even simply lining and then covering across a natural depression in the ground. Drawing: *Missions and Missionaries of California*, via Wikipedia.

Mono Indians built this hasty brush-pile wikiup to serve while they harvested wild grains. Nothing complicated here! Photo Edward S. Curtis, courtesy of Library of Congress.

ward or backward. The doorway may face in any direction. For waterproofing, pieces of hide are thrown over the outer thatching, and in rainy weather, if a fire is not needed, even the smoke hole is covered. In warm, dry weather much of the outer roofing is stripped off. It takes approximately three days to erect a sturdy dwelling of this type. These houses are "warm and comfortable, even though there is a big snow." The interior is lined with brush and grass beds over which robes are spread . . .

In a survival situation where the plan is to get home, one may or may not want to dedicate three days to building a shelter—but you will note that in the description of how this shelter was built, there is no mention of the use of tools except for a digging stick. The time spent building a rude shelter is at least directly proportional to its dimension, and the same architecture and materials can often be built man-size in a disproportional fraction of the time that would be required by a larger and structurally more complex version.

The "ribs" of this Apache wikiup in Arizona ca. 1880 bear a striking resemblance to Mesolithic structures found in Ireland and Paleolithic structures found in the Ukraine. Obviously the Ukrainians didn't teach the Irish, who in turn did not teach the Apache. Men in every time period, in every venue, did what worked for shelter. Whether you build this a size that you can just crawl into, the size of a pup tent, or the size of a camp trailer depends on your situation. But after tens of thousands of years, this sort of hut still goes up quickly and does the job. Photo: N.H. Rose, via Wikipedia.

This Apache wikiup from the turn of the 20th century would have been seasonal shelter, readily built from local materials with no tools. A miniature, hasty version would serve a "survivor" very well overnight. Photo: Edward S. Curtis, courtesy of Library of Congress.

A Cowichan woman from British Columbia harvests tule reeds, which will be used to build dwellings, mats, and furnishings. Depending on the venue, you can quickly likewise gather cattail stalks, cane (bamboo), creosote bush stems, cactus ribs, yucca flower stalks, evergreen boughs, bulrushes, and various flower stalks. Any long, reasonably straight plant will weave into coarse or fine mats for bedding, roofing, thatch, or walls. In the photo below left see how tule reeds are woven into a temporary but snug hut where the reed comprises both the walls and the thatch. Photo: Edward S. Curtis, courtesy of Library of Congress.

A Pomo wikiup of tule reeds serves seasonally while the inhabitants harvest and dry lake fish. Photo: Edward S. Curtis, courtesy of Library of Congress.

A hasty wikiup can be not much more than a brush pile with a hole inside if you have something on top to turn the water. Inhabitants apparently set up this hasty camp while harvesting local acorns. Photo: Edward S. Curtis, courtesy of Library of Congress.

This Chemehuevi house in the northwest Mojave Desert is built of straight brush common along sandy washes and is held in place by mounded dirt. The lesson: use what you have. Photo: Edward S. Curtis, courtesy of Library of Congress.

This Cahuilla house in a California desert was probably a seasonal abode, but it even featured a windbreak, all from materials at hand. Photo: Edward S. Curtis, courtesy of Library of Congress.

Paviotso wikiup at Walker Lake, Nevada, was built near sources of native grains for seasonal use. Photo: Edward S. Curtis, courtesy of Library of Congress.

Spacious Wichita grass lodge may be the "grass hut" in its finest form, illustrating what master craftsmen can do with native materials. Bundles or bunches of grass can also be used in small, crude shelters. Photos: Edward S. Curtis, courtesy of Library of Congress.

A Skokomish portable house sheathed in reed mat from the Pacific Northwest about the turn of the 20th century. Although such a painstaking endeavor would not be a practical project in a survival scenario, this illustrates the adaptability of such materials as cedar bark strips and native reeds and grasses. Photo: Edward S. Curtis, courtesy of Library of Congress.

A wikiup is built and abandoned. A wigwam, shown here, usually has components such as the grass-mat or hide covering removed and relocated on the next wigwam. For short-to-medium-term survival, think wikiup: quick and crude but life-saving shelter. Photo: Edward S. Curtis, courtesy of Library of Congress.

The final development of the wigwam was the better-designed tepee, all of which was worth moving to the next location. If there were no skins or European canvas available, tepees were covered with woven mats of reeds and grass. Pictured is a Yakima mat tepee from about the turn of the 20th century. Photo: Edward S. Curtis, courtesy of Library of Congress.

This Pima ki, built from arrow brush and dirt, would last a long time in the arid Arizona climate. For on-the-move survival, you can use the same materials and techniques to build a shelter not much larger than a man, which could be done quickly and would work just fine. Other materials in other climes can follow the same architecture. Photo: Edward S. Curtis, courtesy of Library of Congress.

The distinction between a wikiup and hogan can blur, depending on how substantial and permanent it is. This Havasupai wikiup of brush, reeds, and earth comes close to being a proper hogan. Photo: Edward S. Curtis, courtesy of Library of Congress.

CHAPTER 7

HOGANS, SOD, AND EARTH SHELTERS

WARMTH WITHOUT WOOD

Flat or angular stones make excellent, fast components, even for a hasty shelter, because with a little stone stem wall it's just a matter of dimension between an ad hoc, sleeping-bag-sized hut and a solid base for a wikiup or a basic hogan. Natives in the American Southwest built hogan-style shelters with only the most basic Neolithic tools, from adobe, earth, timber, twigs, brush, cactus ribs, reeds, and stone. Where good stone was available, the structures still stand. Hogan building has not been completely abandoned even today. The hogans are warm, cool, and doable with what is at hand.

A classic Navajo hogan (next page) is adapted to the setting. Digging down gives a head start on building up, so most hogans start with an excavation, situated where water will not run in. They have thick, tapered walls built from a combination of earth, stone, and adobe, architecturally like earth-sheltered houses in pre-medieval Europe. They usually have a domed roof built of similar materials, built on a framework of timbers.

SOD AS SHELTER

Historians who hazard such guesses say there once were more than a million sod houses on the American frontier. Most sod houses were built for lack of conventional materials, lack of tools, or both, but if you had an ax, a shovel, or a long knife, you could build something out of sod. The most common reason for

Builders of this Arizona high-country hogan had access to small logs and timbers, so they built luxuriously tall in order to save digging into rocky ground. Photo: Edward S. Curtis, courtesy of Library of Congress.

This classic Navajo hogan, built in a low area of the Sonoran Desert in Cañon del Muerta, illustrates how digging in eliminates the need to build up, the thrifty use of wood, and the luxurious use of soft soil—i.e., the logical use of local conditions and materials. Photo: Edward S. Curtis, courtesy of Library of Congress.

building sod houses was the lack of timber in the American Great Plains and Canadian Prairies. Many, especially in home-steaded lands, were intended to provide shelter with what was available, so that later a log or sawn-lumber, stone, or brick house could be built. Many were built to a very high standard, plastered inside and out and used for generations. Some were quick-and dirty for temporary use and did not last.the

Sod house built into a side hill in 1880, by frontier photographer Solomon D. Butcher, from cut sod and found wood. Photo: Courtesy National Park Service.

The fastest way into the shelter of a permanent sod house was the basic dugout, using an existing hill for at least one wall and often part of roof. Posing in summer of 1886 at their home-stead near Sargent, Nebraska, were Emma and Sylvester Rawding, and children Bessie, Philip, William, and Harry. Mules are seen at right, while a cow grazed on the roof. This writer's mother was born in such a dugout on the Saskatchewan prairie in 1911—alas too far north to grow watermelon. Photo: Solomon D. Butcher, courtesy of Library of Congress.

This Ukrainian-style burdei is a dugout-style sod house, here re-created at a Ukrainian Cultural Heritage Village in Alberta. Unless you have decided to winter over, a temporary "survival" situation would not warrant such a timber-framed, solid structure, but what is of interest to our study here is the way the roofing sod has been used, so it will shed water. Even in a quick, temporary shelter the size of a coffin, the sod or other material is arranged to turn water. Photo: Wikipedia.

As shown by this reconstructed "earth lodge" at Glenwood, Iowa, even when abundant forest and plant materials are available, American natives of the upper Midwest (e.g., the Mandan, the Hidatsa, and the Arikara) who were farmers and traders, often used wood-framed, earth-sheltered homes because they were simply the most practical. Settlements of up to a thousand such homes were a familiar sight to frontier traders and explorers along the banks of the Little Missouri. The lesson? Use all materials at hand for a quick survival shelter, and don't overlook common soil. Photo: Wikipedia.

DIG A QUIGGLY HOLE

The "quiggly hole," also known simply as a quiggly or kekuli, was an underground house built by the indigenous people of the interior of British Columbia and the Columbia Plateau in central Washington, and at some locations along the Pacific Northwest Coast. "Quiggly" is a corruption of kickwillie or keekwulee, the Chinook trade language word for "beneath" or "under."

Most were dug to depth, then roofed with timbers, and domed with earth. In some locations there is evidence of hundreds of these dwellings, which could have housed a thousand or more people. As we have seen, the earth itself is good shelter: even a shallow trench scooped out in a suitable location or a natural depression covered with forest rubble can be warm shelter for a night or more.

In interesting juxtaposition, poly-wrapped hay bales lie in a field behind old sod agricultural sheds in Iceland. Sod is a good native building material, even if it lacks respectability. Photo: Christian Bickel, via Wikipedia.

This hut on the Selawik River in Alaska uses it all: driftwood, sod, stones, and brush—even a flotsam door—which were all found materials. Unless you decide to stay, you might not build so permanently, but the lesson is this: press into quick service whatever has floated your way. Photo: Edwards S. Curtis, courtesy of Library of Congress.

SNOW

BRICK AND MORTAR OF THE ARCTIC CIRCLE

The Aleut and Inuit have many names for snow; to one whose world is made up of snow, it is important to distinguish between the various forms.

The best types of snow to use for building an igloo are snow that has been blown by wind (which tends to compact and interlock the ice crystals) and mature snow (which tends to stick together). The hole left in the snow where the blocks are cut is usually used as the lower half of the shelter, which serves as a cold-air sump. A short tunnel is constructed at the entrance to reduce wind and heat loss when the door is opened. Because of the excellent insulating properties of snow, inhabited igloos are surprisingly comfortable and warm inside. A single block of clear ice can be used for a light window. Natives used skins as door flaps. When used as winter shelters, igloos had beds made of snow, covered with twigs and caribou skins.

The igloo is unique in that it is a dome that can be raised out of independent blocks leaning on each other and fit together without any supporting structure during construction. A properly built igloo will support the weight of a man on the roof. In a traditional Inuit igloo, the heat from the kudlik (stone lamp) can slightly melt the interior surface, and this melting and refreezing forms a layer of ice that increases the strength of the dome.

The sleeping platform is raised and tends to hold heat generated by a stove, lamp, or inhabitants. The Central Inuit, es-

Materials for shelter are everywhere. Nearly a hundred years ago, Frank Kleinschmidt recorded Eskimos building a family-size, seasonal igloo (top). Once completed, they donned traditional finery and invited the photographer and his wife (bottom) for a company dinner of frozen crab. A one-or-two-man shelter can be quickly built. Photos: Frank E. Kleinschmidt, courtesy of Library of Congress.

pecially those around the Davis Strait, lined the living area with skins, which could increase the temperature from just above freezing to a temperate 50–68 degrees Fahrenheit.

For the 1922 documentary *Nanook of the North*, an Inuit named Allakariallak built a large family igloo as well as a smaller igloo for sled dogs, using an ivory knife to cut and trim snow blocks, as well as the clear ice for a window, in about an hour. That igloo would house five people.

The usefulness, and structural integrity, of the igloo de-

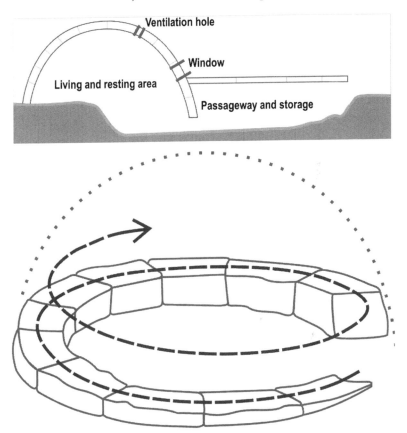

The user-friendly design of the igloo features a sump to keep cold air down and living/sleeping quarters higher, where warm air collects. The clever spiral erection technique allows one man to build a strong dome structure. Drawings: Anuskafm, courtesy Wikipedia.

pends on very specific design principles. As seen on the previous page and below, the layout is based on sound architectural precepts, and the methodology and sequence of construction allow it to be erected by one man.

A modern Eskimo builds an igloo in Cape Dorset (southern region of Baffin Island). The clothing is now synthetic and the knife steel instead of bone, but the timeless architectural design and materials will not be changed until it can be improved. Photo: by Ansgar Walk, courtesy Wikipedia.

BUILDING A QUINZHEE

The snow used for a quinzhee is not as particular as for an igloo; it just needs to be of such a consistency that it will pack. An OK quinzhee is also more readily built by a rank amateur, although it is not as suitable for permanent shelter, nor can it be safely built as large as an igloo. Although conceptually similar, a quinzhee is less sturdy than an igloo but can be a favorable tradeoff where there is no igloo-suitable snow. A shovel is not an absolute necessity, but you will need something better than hands to scoop, move, and pack snow.

The method of construction is to pile the snow in a solid

Similar in concept but differing from an igloo in material specifics and building technique, a quinzhee can be a good survival option. Photo: Wikipedia.

heap to the outside dimension of the quinzhee, which is shaped similarly to an igloo but with a more pointed dome, for a hasty shelter about 6 feet high. When within a couple of feet of the outside dimension, put on a layer of marking sticks or dirt, and from that point on the snow must be packed on as tightly as possible. The pile is then left to harden and form new crystals, depending on conditions, in three to eight hours.

When the snow has set up, excavate out the interior to the marking layer of sticks or dirt. A smaller hut-type shelter is more practical as it conserves heat. If you are building alone, it is important to stay on your knees rather than digging from a prone position, in the event of a cave-in. A good method of excavating the interior is to define a block or chunk of snow with the shovel or expedient tool and pry it free. Excavate an interior corridor front to back and then dig out the sides.

This type of structure will not support the weight of a man, but there is enough weight in the snow to suffocate a man, just as in an avalanche, so build no larger than necessary, and be sure snow has properly set. Leave the sides thick because if you accidentally breach the side during excavation, it can all come down. If the snow is at all slushy, it is not suitable for a quinzhee.

I have seen one-man shelters built from the wet snow of the Pacific Northwest by rolling it into balls as if to make a snowman, and stacking these in rows waist high and body wide, to a point in the middle, or building a roof of forest material and covering it with snow.

DIGGING A SNOW CAVE

A snow cave, given the right kind and shape of snow, can have thermal properties similar to an igloo and is particularly effective at providing protection from wind as well as low temperatures. A properly made snow cave can be 32°F or warmer inside, even when the outside temperature is minus 40°F.

As seen in the illustration on the following page from a Department of Defense manual, a snow cave is constructed by excavating snow so the entrance tunnel is lower than the main space, to retain warm air. Construction is simplified by building it on a steep slope and digging slightly upward and horizontally into the slope. The ceiling is domed to prevent dripping on the occupants. Adequate snow depth, free of rocks and ice, is needed (4 or 5 feet). The snow must be compact or consolidated naturally so that it retains its structure. The walls and roof should be at least a foot thick. A small pit may be dug deeper into one part of the cave floor, preferably near the entrance, to provide a place for the coldest air to settle. The entrance may be partially blocked with chunks of snow to block wind and retain heat, although it is vital to prevent drifting snow from completely plugging the entrance, as ventilation is crucial in a confined space.

This is another instance where a digging tool of some sort is vital, as snow soft enough to be scooped out by hand is probably too soft to safely maintain its shape.

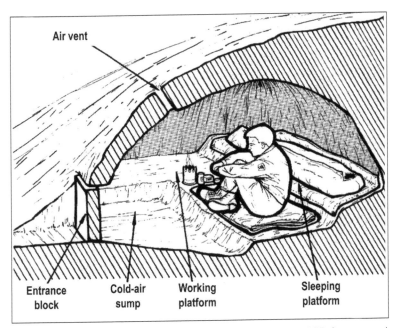

Air vent

Entrance block

Cold-air sump

Working platform

Sleeping platform

Drawing: Department of Defense manual.

APPENDIX

PONCHOS AND PARACHUTES—THE GI WAY

There is no telling how you found yourself in a survival situation, but if you had to punch out or got separated from your unit and have a parachute or a basic GI poncho, there are a number of quick and intuitive shelters that can be made from them. The following drawings and text are adapted from various editions of FM 21-76. In some cases, the text was condensed or considered unnecessary here. Civilian gear such as blankets and tarps may be used in similar fashion. These also have the advantage of no-tool construction.

PONCHO LEAN-TO

Tie off the hood of the poncho. Pull the drawstring tight, roll the hood the long way, fold it into thirds, and tie it off with the drawstring.

On one long side of the poncho, tie a rope to the corner grommet. Tie another to the other corner grommet.

Attach a drip stick a few inches long to each rope about an inch from the grommet. These drip sticks will keep rainwater from running down the ropes into the lean-to. Tying strings a few inches long to each grommet along the poncho's top edge will allow the water to run to and down the line without dripping into the shelter.

Tie the ropes about waist high on the trees (uprights). Use a round turn and two half hitches with a quick-release knot.

Spread the poncho and anchor it to the ground, putting sharpened sticks through the grommets and into the ground.

If you plan to use the lean-to for more than one night or you expect rain, make a center support for the lean-to. Make this support with a line. Attach one end of the line to the poncho hood and the other end to an overhanging branch. Make sure there is no slack in the line. Or, you can place a stick upright under the center of the lean-to. This method, however, will restrict your space and movements in the shelter. For additional protection from wind and rain, place brush or equipment at the open sides of the lean-to. To reduce heat loss to the ground, place insulating material, such as leaves or pine needles, inside.

PONCHO TENT

Tie off the poncho hood in the same way as the poncho lean-to and then tie a rope to the center grommet on each side of the poncho.

Tie the other ends of these ropes at about knee height to two trees several feet apart and stretch the poncho tight.

Draw one side of the poncho tight and secure it to the ground pushing sharpened sticks through the grommets. Follow the same procedure on the other side.

VARIOUS PARACHUTE SHELTERS

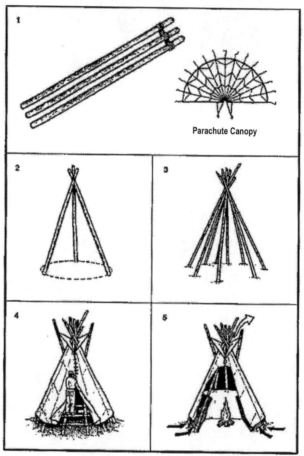

Parachute Canopy

Three-Pole Parachute Tepee

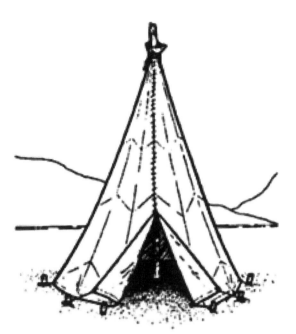

One-Pole Parachute Tepee

No-Pole (Suspended) Parachute Tepee

One-Man Shelter

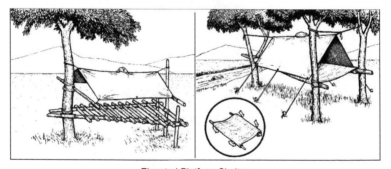

Elevated Platform Shelter

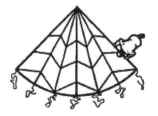

1 Lay out parachute and cut six gores of material.

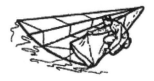

2 Starting from one side, make two folds each, one gore in width, yielding a base of three thicknesses of material.

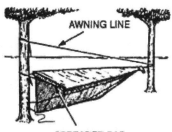

AWNING LINE

SPREADER BAR

3 Suspend hammock between two trees with the skirt higher than the apex.* Place a spreader bar between the lines at the skirt and lace it to the skirt. Stretch an awning line between the two trees.

* An alternate and more stable configuration would be to tie each side of the skirt to a separate tree. However, this configuration of three trees could be difficult to find.

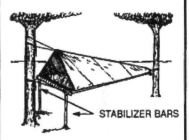

STABILIZER BARS

4 Drape the remaining three gores over the awning line and tuck the sixth gore into the shelter. Prop forked branches under the spreader bar to stabilize the shelter.

Parachute Hammock